GLEANINGS FROM
A CORNISH NOTEBOOK

Dorothy Delancey Nicholls

**First published in 1986
by Dyllansow Truran
Trewolsta, Trewirgie, Redruth, Kernow (Cornwall)**

ISBN 1 85022 025 5

Earles Press, Redruth, Kernow

TRURAN

FOREWORD

Mrs. Dorothy Delancey Nicholls, 1901-1985, a prominent member of the Old Cornwall Society at Lostwithiel, left this little book of studies for posthumous publication.

A founder-member of the Lostwithiel Museum, the author of a book on the Black Prince and of a Guide to Lostwithiel she was a respected local-historian. Her knowledge of Cornish hedges derived in part from her great love of walking - she had walked round the whole of the Cornish coast and virtually no part of our country was unknown to her. It was for her definitive work on Cornish Hedges that she was made a bard of the Cornish Gorsedd, taking as her Bardic name Covathor Keow (the Recorder of Hedges).

The studies here published reflect some of the learning, the warmth and the charm of this dedicated Cornish Lady.

CONTENTS

ILLUSTRATIONS

A GLIMPSE OF SMUGGLING

Immediately overlooking the quay at Lostwithiel stands Norway House. The imposing late Georgian building, with the unusual feature of two wings, was strategically sited above a garden 50 yards wide, sloping down to quay level. Thus was Captain Norway assured of concealed access to his impressive vaulted cellars. On retirement from the East India Company in 1753, Captain Norway, great great uncle of Nevil Shute Norway, the author, planned the entire outlay.

But regretfully the Captain, whose masterly plan was to have rewarded him with a new way of life, died in 1757 before the building was completed. "A very wealthy man," writes his great great nephew. The Captain had no son. In his will the whole was bequeathed in trust to his nephew, Nevel (sic) Norway, then aged 17, with a request that he continue to carry out the plan. Nevel Norway, a competent young man, had the house and cellars completed before he came of age in 1761. We may imagine the long and fruitful talks between uncle and nephew disclosing the motive in the siting and foreplanning.

In 1763 Nevel Norway married Sarah Arthur, daughter of John Arthur of the Crown and Sceptre in Lostwithiel. By then he was accepted by the town as Merchant and Banker. In the 18th century the appellation "merchant," albeit with no visible sign of merchandise, proved acceptable, and presumed respectability. As Banker, Nevel Norway, with innate aptitude, centred his public life on the east wing, having there a direct outdoor entrance. Here above his vaulted cellars, with a massive safe, he reigned supreme. Later he became Mayor of Lostwithiel, had a large family, and died in 1814. He was laid to rest in the family vault under the aisle of the church.

May we now with hindsight, guided by family letters and records set down the findings?

Along the quayside the garden is bounded by a low stone wall, two to three feet high. From the entrance gate, the drive runs parallel to the wall to the furthest corner of the garden.

Here, under two feet of soil, a level platform of stone, six feet square was discovered. This was presumably the landing stage for "tubs." Even the remaining course of the drive falls into place, being angled at the landing stage to run diagonally towards the house. Tubs were carried along this drive to a low doorway in the east wing. Within was a sorting space and two granite stairways. Of these one led up to the Bank, the other, a spiral stair, to the house.

An arched entrance led eastward, which brings to light a further motive in Captain Norway's adoption of the particular site. Parallel with the east wing at 60 yards distance runs South Street. Down one side, under a granite culvert, runs the small river Cober, dividing Lostwithiel parish from the country parish of Lanlivery. This water course thus ensured complete freedom from any jurisdiction raised by Lostwithiel.

Under the long archway at the rear of the Stannary building the culvert fills the entire space leaving no side track. To overcome this obstacle the Captain planned a tunnel. So the arched entrance leading eastward from the sorting space is eight feet high, and leads into a tunnel of the same height. This passage runs four feet underground toward South Street. Well built and arched throughout it runs beneath the stables and under two back gardens for 60 yards before reaching South Street at ground level. It rose, now hidden under a heavy mantle of ivy, on unused land. I was shown a length of passage by a young man building a greenhouse directly above.

Through the second arched doorway one enters the cellars. Here sixteen pillars stand in rows of four. All are ten feet high, of red brick, with capital and base of granite. Between the pillars four wide passages lead away into darkness, quaywards, in either sidewall are set three rows of wine bins, each with arched roof, blending with the vaulted roof of the cellar.

Vaulted Cellar.
'NORWAY HOUSE'
LOSTWITHIEL.
Oct. 197

The sorting of tubs took place beneath the wing. Tubs to go north went through the underground passage. Those for farmers to the courtyard before the east wing. These would have been cleared by night or before sunrise. The rest were stored in the cellars. Each tub weighed 36lbs., and contained four gallons of brandy. In 1775 Nevel Norway took over the King's Arms Inn. At a Mayor's dinner held at the Arms, 89lbs beef at 3¾ pence a lb. and nine quarts of brandy at 5/4d a gallon were consumed.

Since 1690 the Norways had been established in Lostwithiel. Nevel Shute Norway, writing of his great great uncle says "a grand old man, much respected in the town. I have two bank notes of Nevel's Bank, unissued, of £5 each, dated 1805."

A Glimpse of Smuggling

The smuggling trade through Norway House was run on a financially sound basis with two families in Guernsey. The enterprise was clearly designed to take advantage of the Early Charters held by Guernsey which exempted her from paying revenue to British Customs. When George III found himself short of revenue during the Napoleonic Wars, he renewed efforts to impose Customs and Excise officers on Guernsey. Relying on their Charters, Guernsey refused. In 1767 Customs and Excise managed to attain a precarious foothold in Jersey and Guernsey. But they were later routed, in fact 1775 became known as the Golden age of smuggling.

The families who shared the enterprise with Norway House, the Priaulx and the Tuppers (related to Victor Hugo), lived overlooking St. Peter Port where many of the vaults were under their command.

Now came the discovery of the subtle improvements in flavour of wines and spirits matured in the caves under the climate of Guernsey. This led to the opening of a regular and facile route between that Channel Island and Cornwall.

The Priaulx traded directly with Roscoff: the Norways then traded directly with Guernsey. As a precedent, the trafficking between Lanlivery and Guernsey, run on successful business lines, may reveal a glimpse "as the gentlemen go by."

A cargo of brandy cost £1500 in Guernsey and sold in Britain for £3000. A gallon cost 3/3d smuggled, but 5/4d over a counter.

When the ancestral home in a parish provided the finance, captain and crew were never lacking. On the word Captain would hire a boat for £150, also £100 to pay 4 crewmen £25 each. Then £1 per tub was banked to cover expenses.

Even before landing the galley was recognised by knowing men and women on farms on the cliffs, especially one farm overlooking Polmear. On nearing the entrance to Fowey harbour, the cutter drew in towards the small bay. Here two deep steps have been cut into the rock face providing a smuggler, loaded with a tub, means to make his way to the long tunnel in the south cliff which led under the fields to the farmhouse above. The tunnel opened in the dairy. From the farm a field path led with all appearance of innocence, down to the roadway, where conveniently stood the Ship Inn.

If the way were clear to slip into the harbour, signals having been exchanged as to "strangers" being about, rowers took their cargo up the river. The goods weighed several tons. To compete with the shallow river, at the first creek smugglers transferred their cargo to barges. Word went swiftly round. Farmers were waiting at many creeks upstream. After dark goods were unloaded at short quays. Nightfall was the favoured time for landings. On drawing up to the quay the Captain landed and took his stance. Beside him stood a man with a lantern, his back to the wind. All was quiet and orderly. The men were bonded by trust and there were no loafers nor drunkards among them. A joke which scored off the Excise men was greeted with high glee.

Smuggling called for men who were athletic and muscular, with presence of mind and who welcomed risks. The Cornish, being Celtic, had that innate romanticism and were acknowledged in the smuggling world for their lack of viciousness and brutality. During summer months miners often formed part of the crew. To travel over to Guernsey or even Roscoff, would have provided the essentials their way of life lacked.

With the assured protection from families of standing as here, the nineteen farmers on the estate soon showed a reckless daring. Indeed Squire as J.P., M.P. was conversant with every form of rescue. In 1788 Capt. John Carter, the widely heralded "King of Prussia," was sheltered by Lanlivery though £300 was offered for his apprehension. He came to rest with a sorely injured eye. Leeches had failed. A doctor operated. After six days the King of Prussia, much relieved, returned to "duties" unapprehended.

Squire Nicholas Kendall of Pelyn in Lanlivery, though the house is Elizabethan, had cellars under the entire house. Although under two miles inland, his connections with the Norways soon became unmistakeable.

A great uncle of the writer, Osmond Priaulx, made many journeys from Guernsey, between 1870 and 1890, staying at Norway

House or with his cousin Nicholas Kendall at Pelyn. He recounted how landings took place at nightfall. A landing at Lanlivery quay could amount to fifteen tons of goods, tea and spirits. Being essentially a country parish silks were seldom of the cargo.

As word preceeded the landings, ponies were loaned or borrowed unknown. A cousin named Barry, aged 95 in 1970 remembered staying with her uncle, Frank Kendall at Lanlivery vicarage in 1885. He would come in to breakfast rumbling with rage. "The horses were left groomed and fed. Now they are out there covered with mud." One morning he came in beaming. There was a tub of brandy in the stable! An old man who lived near Fowey harbour as a boy, told me his mother spotted a smugglers' cutter unfailingly. He would be sent out to row over with bottles of "lemonade" if accosted, and returned, his bottles well filled with spirits.

Finally there are three sequences that comply with this glimpse of the smuggling world. On 8th of May, 1863 Nicholas Kendall married Claire de Lancey Priaulx.

When air traffic began to grow, Roscoff with her vaults and cellars was chosen as the port of trade.

In 1973 the Western Morning News reported that "the last remaining Customs Officer was being withdrawn from Guernsey because of shortage of Customs and Excise in England. They were first sent to Guernsey in 1805 to stamp out smuggling."

TREES AND THE CORNISH ELM

The sweep of the wind over the hills and the granite subsoil below leave us the bare landscape that is most of Cornwall. Only in the valleys, where the soil has silted and held, trees will root and spread to their full breadth. One long and beautiful stretch of dark woodland lines the lower reaches of the river Fowey after leaving the bare moorlands. Further down to the west on the peninsula leading to St. Michael Penkivel, the soil through centuries of silting from the hills, has enough depth to grow the finest trees in Cornwall. There they grow to their full breadth and girth. High hedges line the narrow roads and a quiet prevails in the hush that trees produce, the wind stirring their branches.

In the game parks round the ancestral homes, oak and chestnut thrive. Here there is always an underlay of bushes, often laurel and rhododendron, providing cover for game, the young birds reared with long-acquired knowledge and patience by their keepers. Arrows of light pierce the dark cover. Hawks are kept at bay.

Water meadows, never ploughed, where cattle graze, give a fine stance and sheltered hold for trees. Here they grow singly, the oaks having grown literally for centuries. With all our hearts we hope they will never be felled.

At last we come to Cornwall's native tree, the tree that bends to all our needs - the Cornish Elm.

Wherever there is a row of trees forming a windbreak on a hill ridge in Cornwall, or an avenue leading to a farm, or "raced along" beside a country road, those trees will be Cornish elms. Growing happily in the warm damp climate, and on light shallow soil, they are indigenous to Cornwall. They have neither the brittleness, nor the tendency to internal decay of the English elm. Nor does the fungus grow, nor the scolytus beetle attack them.

The silhouette is slender and graceful with a tufted plume of leaves that are smaller than those of the English elm. The trunk is upright with a lasting suppleness. The branches lead at an upward angle, and, ideally for timber, at a high point. This gives the tree a pliancy well suited to a hilltop setting. A single row of Cornish elms will sway easily to winds that would bend heavier trees.

In the bareness of winter the belt of Cornish elms that shelter farmhouses and buildings from north and east winds, stand out on the skyline. Their perfect silhouettes are striking in winter. Their extreme suppleness has meant a strong link with tradition in Cornwall. The pilot gigs that worked from the Scillies and the Lizard before the days of steam were built solely of wood from Cornish

6

elms. No other tree could yield a 28 foot plank so fine and thin that it will ripple like a ribbon when held at one end. The six-oared gigs, though weighing seven to eight hundredweight are so flexible that a grip at bow or stern can shudder the gig from end to end. In their pliancy the gigs give to the wind. One writes in the present tense, but steam has ousted the gigs from their right as pilot boats. They are used now only for racing at Newquay and in the Scillies.

The old-time gigs lie foresaken in dark boathouses, or even in hidden shallows of the creeks. Very few are seaworthy, and the undertakings of those few are as dark as their lairs.

CORNISH STONEHEDGING

Where lies the true heart of Cornwall? It lies in her granite, her minerals, strong, beautiful and unyielding. This is revealed to those who walk. They become aware of the variety of stone used by the Cornish stonehedgers in building the field walls. The age of these walls ranges from the Bronze Age to the 19th Century, giving an air of stability and strength to the landscape.

The walls hold the key to the natural features of each part of the country. The hedger uses the stone that rises to hand. This may be granite, ironstone, slate or sandstone or quartz.

The earliest enclosed fields are found near Zennor, where the pre-historic Beaker folk landed. Caches of flints, axe-heads and Bronze Age pottery have been found beneath the walling.

Above the road stands Zennor Tor. From the sea of boulders strewn beneath the tor, stones weighing up to half a ton faced the little Beaker folk. Using wood levers, working always downhill, they upended the boulders from their setting and rolled them down. Standing on end, each boulder was balanced against its neighbour with lesser stones wedged between them. Thus were the small enclosures formed.

Too small for cultivation by tractor, these sparse fields, apparently as bare as the clifftops, are the favoured habitat of Guernsey cattle, their coats sleek and shining. The acid soil, sea air and richly mineralized land ensures that gleam of health in their coats. Let us recall where the breed originated - Guernsey! Farmers have proved that, moved to other land, they will lose their fine condition.

Cropping has to be light from lack of depth in the soil. Pony and hand work grows bulbs, brassica and potatoes.

In one field a farmer, determined to keep his sheep within bounds, hobbled them by tying each foreleg to the hind leg with old rope, leaving them reduced to a flounder at sight of a walker or a dog. Cattle and sheep ignore those who go by in cars "missing so much and so much."

To bar animals from leaving the fields, cattle grids of three granite bars are laid over a shallow pit, or there is a stile of granite steps. The gateways are merely an iron bar laid across spaced boulders. The bar is often worn to an open channel, which gives one an idea of the effect the saltladen winds would have on timber gates. The sheep field had two bars.

The fields above the Zennor to Penzance road are larger and suited to sheep. The stones are less unwieldy and the walls only five feet high. But the loose way of building has left interstices of daylight throughout their length. This alone defeats the rebellious ewe, who sees them as precarious and retires. Though standing on higher ground and swept by still harsher gales, these walls stand by virtue of sifting the winds.

Further round the Atlantic coast, near St. Just-in-Penwith and Cape Cornwall, there is some superb walling. It runs straight as a bee-line round each side of the large rectangular fields. The walls were built soon after the Enclosure Act 1760 allowed the strips and stitches of mediaeval days to be enclosed in fields. We may date them as contemporary with tin-mining.

Along the six foot wide foundation large basal stones are set. On these the seven foot height is achieved with eight or nine parallel rows of ironstone. These stones were to be collected from around the heads of the mineshafts, after the tin lode had been extracted by the hammers of the "Bal maidens," working round the mineheads. The arsenical content of the stones keeps the walls white and weed free. The only growth on them in over two centuries is the grass on the two feet wide cope. The hearting of the walls is of small stones. To those who love Cornwall there comes a thrill of pride in the country skill that built the walls.

To see the widest of all Cornish hedges we go on the cliffs above Padstow. Here huge seas rush in, bursting upward in soaring sheets of spray. The walls were built in 1730 to conform with the earliest Enclosure Acts. At first we see a wall of thick slate stones set in vertical rows, with a five feet fall and perfect batter. The cope, set at an angle, juts outward to throw off water. But walk over near the wall to see its astonishing breadth. The cope is a pathway of slate stone along which two people may walk abreast.

Pink thrift blows along its length, and over the side sea-campion foams - an unforgettable image of rough-hewn strength and softening beauty. Through innumerable winters, sheep and lambs have lain under the protection of these walls. The shelter they yield in yards is equal to four times their height. The massive bulwarks stand immune against all savage gales.

The widest part of the north coast of Cornwall is sheep country par excellence. Here is hedging peculiar to Tintagel. The large thirty acre fields are bounded with apparently solid stone walls. They are in reality stone-faced hedges, neatly and effectively faced with patterned stonework. The slate, native to Tintagel, is so easily split with a hand tool that a hedger can cut squares of nine inches as fast as a quarryman. Over a hearting of small stones and turf, the sides are faced with the hand-cut slates set in close rows. Each row slants alternately with the row above, forming the "Kersey" way, or sometimes "Jack and Jill." A man's labour was, and is, six yards a day; eight yards can just be achieved, but the hedger retires exhausted.

As these field walls are only five feet high, to deter the ever-enquiring "break-dance" ewe, sharp-cut stones, one to two feet, roughly halfmoon are set on the cope. On hillsides the cope slopes upward, their weight holding the stones firm. A stone dislodged from the downward slope carries its fellows with it.

Above Boscastle quite different stone lies on and below ground. Fields are wide and treeless on the clifftops. Screaming seabirds wheel and swoop into the caves below. On this hard land foundations are set with boulders of quartz, hard as marble and as impossible to split. On these, with a hearting of fine loam soil, blue elvant slate stone catches even the eye of a motorist flashing past. On the cope larger stones set to jut outward, not only to throw off lashings of spray, sea water and rain, but to dotor tho rebel ewe who faces an overhang she cannot leap, and dangers she cannot see.

Near Tintagel, Boscastle and Port Quin there are some delightful aspects of sheep care - the sheep-creeps. In the fields overlooking the sea, during Spring and Summer sheep and lambs can

Slate stone walls,
found near quarries.

come out through the creeps to crop the short sweet grass of the clifftops, which is ideal for young lambs. As the field walls are six feet through at the base, the creeps built into them are virtually passages. The creep opening is four feet high and three feet wide. The sides are built up and the roof is of flat slate stone. The floor is paved with heavy slate to ensure the continual tread of cloven

*Slate with longstone to bind, gives
shelter over field to four times
the height. Boscastle.*

hooves shall not form a pocket of water undermining the whole. Worked to blend with each particular form of walling, the stonehedger could well have stood back and admired his own craftmanship.

When autumn arrives the farmer blocks the passage by rolling a large boulder into the creep. He takes a further precaution. Out on the cliff-edge, at intervals of eight to ten feet, he sinks slate stone uprights one third of their height into the turf. Standing then four feet high, a set of holes are bored and three lines of thick wire run through them. They deter sheep from the perilous edge of the cliff. Even so, I fear one does sometimes see a still white form lying far below.

From the backbone of Cornwall, let us now go down on her soft greener parts. Here on the south coast the winds are less strong, the hodges are built more loosely, and low bushes are rooted in the hearting. Hedge flowers have found a footing, and tho stonework is overgrown and green. Plant roots bind the walling. In cliffside fields below Lansallos, clever walls defeat not only sheep but cattle. The sloping land caused a further method to be used. Over a hearting of earth and shale the walls are built up to shoulder height and six feet wide. The stones are then set in panels four feet wide, alternately vertical and horizontal. On the cope overhanging slate flagstones, each four feet square have been set in *pairs* the whole length of the wall. They thus form a table with the deterring overhang of a foot on ,either side. Neither sheep nor bullock could clear them. The rebellious ewe seeking a loose stone or a gap with her nose would be baffled. If a bullock improbably gained the top, it would be checkmated by the outward view. A bullock cannot take off as would a horse. It will only slither down a slope.

This is softer land so the birds and flowers comply. Out on the water cormorants take over the rocks, drying their outspread wings. During flowering months many uncommon little blooms are there beside the pathways.

Cornish stonehedging shows still more variations, though less striking perhaps. On the moorland farms high dry stonehedging without turf hearting forms the boundary wall between the farms. With a fall of five to six feet, they stand as built 200 years ago. Each stone rests firmly on or against its neighbour. Small stones form the centre and form wedges on the outer surface. Moorland winds brook of no crevices of soil; the walls are of clean granite. Built apparently haphazardly the stonecraft is there.

Near some slate quarries there are fields simply enclosed with rectangular slabs of slate with three feet below ground. The slabs stand four to five feet above, shoulder to shoulder, occasionally with iron bonding, well rusted, at the back.

In some Boscastle walls there are binders set to hold vertical uprights.

Through the walls surrounding gameparks there are tunnels running through, about eighteen inches from the ground. They run every eight to twelve feet, are roofed with slate, roughly paved and having a well built entrance on either side. Through these 'rabbit boxes' rabbits could enter and leave the gameparks without the game escaping. Nor did they then need to undermine the walling to gain the park. All the young shoots of brambles were nipped literally in the bud by their chewing. The woods were thus cleared of undergrowth.

Sandstone is used in the method of stonepanelling that we find where the walls shore up the hilly roads in towns. We see this in walls descending into Fowey, Truro and North Hill.

One can understand the way stonehedging grew and fitted into the awakening of the whole landscape. The insect life born there benefits the land. The mineral of each area comes to the surface.

I began a study of the field walls while walking round the coastline. Interest grew until it became imperative not to leave a single type unexamined, to deduce the mineral of each district from the stone used, to appraise the various methods of building, and to appreciate how wind, weather and livestock were taken into account. They served to form a glorious challenge that bonded together all the Cornishmen wresting a living from their native land.

Jagged slate cope on
Kersey way walling. Tintagel.

THE FASCINATION OF OLD DOCUMENTS

Leaving the world of 1985 with its hurry and bustle, where words are abbreviated and mispronounced, and often reduced to a string of initials, we are entering another world, a world of leisure, of careful modes of expression, of quaint spelling and of beautiful penmanship, the world of old manuscripts. The word derives from the latin *manu* (by hand) and *scriptus* (written). I want to show the interest to be found in them and how rewarding the study of them proves.

Before 1830 all writing was with a goose quill pen, cut and slit by the writer with his penknife, to suit his hand. Therefore knowing the care that went into their making and the fragile nature of the paper, we handle them gently unfolding slowly so that cracks and creases shall not form. As one bends over there rises a musty smell taking us into that old world. The paper may be frayed at the edges, the ink fading but the capital letters are swirling beautifully and the panmanship clear and even. The wording may be curious; Dr. Johnson, too hefty and fat to ride a Highland pony, says he is "incommoded by corpulence." In spelling we find "cup board" in two words, giving a picture of the array of pewter mugs displayed on a sideboard. Old manuscripts and documents are legion. We will take four examples.

(1) The most likely source of old handwritten papers are letters, diaries and accounts, revealing the day to day life of our great-great-grandfathers; not only the lives but the temperament of the writer. In the Bodleian Library at Oxford there are preserved, under glass, letters from men and women famous in the 19th century. A letter from Shelley reveals a passionate impulsive nature, racing untidily across the page. Beside it is the precise accurate writing of Addison the classic essayist, and Jane Austen's letter, neat and restrained. The most charming is a letter from Kenneth Graham, author of 'Wind in the Willows,' to his little son continuing a bedtime story, described with small drawings in the margin, a gypsy seated on an upturned pail peeling potatoes. Each letter matches one's image of the writer.

Here is a letter written in 1847 by my grandfather to his solicitors in a small fine hand with a generous slope. You will notice the graceful wording.

16

"My dear Sir,

Will you have the goodness to cause to be paid, through your London Bankers, twenty pounds to my son's account, as he writes me that he needs a little help at this moment. I fear he is a little extravagent, though I believe the distress he sees around him in his constant patrols, helps to keep him poor.

Believe me, my dear Sir,

Yours sincerely"

Here is an entry from a diary kept by an estate agent who lived at Castle in Lostwithiel in 1810.

"Rose at 3.30 to walk to Fowey to hire a horse to ride to Plymouth to catch a stage coach to London. For which the fare is 10/- or 2/6 more for a seat inside if the weather is inclement."

The coach took three days. I have walked the path he took. As far as Golant a road; from Golant to Fowey a deep-cut path, a smuggler's path hiding man and horse. We would consider that a feat worth showing on television.

Two incidents give us an idea of a sea battle in those days. "A man was cut in two by a cannon ball. His body was blown into the water but strange to tell his legs were left standing on the deck with all the firmness and animation of life."

Then a midshipman was brought into the cockpit with his leg cut off at the calf; he was an herioc youth of 17. Two surgeons could not attend him at that moment. He drew out a knife and cut off a piece of flesh and splinter of bone with great composure. "I can stay" said he, "Let me doctor myself." When the surgeon attended him it was found necessary to amputate above the knee. He submitted to the operation without a groan. (Remember there was no chloroform). "It is nothing at all," he said, "I thought it had been much worse." How wonderful to prove one was descended from that young man.

The despatch of the Duke of Wellington mentions several of his officers. A casualty list contains the name of General Sir William Delancey as severely wounded. He died later after being nursed in a farmhouse. Where we would give transfusion they applied leeches. But the wording was, "He conceived that his wound was mortal."

Most precious and lasting manuscripts are written on parchment or vellum. The elegant carefully formed lettering, the flamboyant exaggerated capitals, the attachment of seals and signatures at the food, all convey the utmost importance of the piece.

They have been painstakingly compiled in legal wordage, by perhaps a clerk seated alone, with only the flame of a candle to warm his hands!

So precious are charters and indentures that they are covered from daylight by a dark cloth. At Merton College Oxford, where law is studied, the tomes are chained to the shelves. They have been thus since the days of Wolsey.

(2) Old account books give all manner of surprises regarding prices. Here is the way a pawn ticket dated 1734 was worded. The draft was in a spidery hand and read "Goods left in pawn with Mrs. Francis Croker of Lostwithiel as a security for the sum of one diamond ring 01-10-0, 2 snuff boxes 01-04-0 received 02-14 shillings for which I leave the above goods as a security, and pledge, and which sum I promise to pay on all demands witness my hand James Beamish."

However one account I actually handled and read was on a scrap of paper preserved since 1649. It was a bill sent in to the Governor of Launceston Gaol by the executioner for his grisly task. It read: "To the execution of six prisoners," and then gave their crimes. I will quote only the first:-

1. for taking one lamb, and added "who upon his examination by force hath confessed. The bill was thus Executions 1-10-0 Drop 1-0 Halter 5-0. The picture it conjures up is horrifying.

(3) The third kind of manuscripts are the social historical. They give a broader view of life, though one does in fact find small personal tragedies. These manuscripts are housed in the County Records Office at Truro, which is warm and spacious, with maps, inventories and records of all kinds. The inventories give the furnishings of houses, the joint stools, rush carpets, four posters and truckle beds and also the apparel (with belt and sovereign purse).

Wills convey a delightful picture as one in 1818: "I give and bequeath to my wife the bed we usually sleep in with stead and furniture thereunto belonging, which she is, can, or otherwise might be entitled to," and another gives a sidelight on a son-in-law: "My said daughter (is) not to be subject to the debts or control, disposition or engagement of her present or any future husband."

Then there are the parish records of the burdens of Overseers of the Pool in 1766 where we find the truth that lay under old nursery rhymes as Little Boy Blue. In the days before schools children were taken as apprentices on farms from the "age of 7 until 21 or the day of marriage." By 1807 these cardings were signed by two Overseers and a J.P. Here is an entry concerning a child pauper which pathetically reads: "A bastard child aged about 7¼ hath intruded herself in your said Parish there to inhabit contrary to Law, and likely chargeable to the Parish of Liskeard. Her legal place of settlement is St. Neot. We therefore order one of you do forthwith remove and convey the said Jane Jago from Liskeard to said Parish of St. Neot." Little Jane had walked to Liskeard with her grandmother who was going to live in the workhouse.

Now for a more cheerful note, here is an account of Preventive men searching for contraband brandy. They came to a farm at Polperro, where the quick-witted farmer's wife took the pins out of her hair, rolled her eyes and gibbered until they fled, leaving her seated on a keg of brandy!

(4) The fourth kind of old papers are not strictly manuscripts, but are so full of interest that I have included them. These are newspapers. In my own collection I have two early copies of the Times. The first one was published on November 7th, 1805 giving the report of the Battle of Trafalgar. The other copy carried news of the Battle of Waterloo and was dated June 22nd, 1815. The Times then had only two small pages compared with our thirty now. The paper was fragile and the price 6d. They were becoming very thin at the folds; to preserve them I covered each page in cellophane. This leaves them perfectly readable and virtually indestructable.

Nelson's end is described with genuine feeling and deep regret in a despatch from Admiral Collingwood. Nelson expressed his wish that he might have died in "my own country."

Reading old documents brings to light an eagerness to find more comparisons, and as piece after piece of knowledge is fitted together, as in a jig-saw, the whole picture comes into view and one finds pleasure in the careful handling and study of old manuscripts.

A CORNISH FOLK MUSEUM
LOSTWITHIEL

This museum gives a portrayal of life in a Cornish town before the coming of electricity with its glare and silent efficiency. Often the different way of life of those who visit and those who man as curators bring from either gasps of almost unbelief. Duties are enjoyable in the extreme.

Thirteen years ago the Old Cornwall Society pleaded with its Council for premises suited to a museum. For eight years we received the recurrent answer, "There is nothing in this town to form a museum." At last the old Market House in Fore Street, with its granite entrance and the town prison at the rear, became vacant. A loyal farmer on the Council pointed out our opportunity. We sprang in and were granted "a try."

Immediately a leaflet explaining the idea, with an appeal, was slipped under every doorway. The understanding and intelligence that people displayed in the gifts they brought forward was astonishing. Every exhibit is labelled with the name of the donor, whether loaned or presented. Every article was a part of the life of a native of the town. Nothing has been purchased.

Within four months we were ready to open. The person to perform the initial opening was the Earl of Mount Edgcumbe. His ancestor had presented the town with the building in 1740, while standing as M.P.

In 1973 the Earl and Countess came down as invited. The town was able to show its gratitude. Since then there have been more than 10,000 entries in a succession of visitor's books. There is something to interest visitors of all ages. Being open for ten days at Easter, followed by a long session from mid May until the end of September and asking only for donations, we thrive not only financially, but in providing delighted appreciation.

Directly above the Market House is the Guildhall. Between Court sessions there, in 1770, a school for law students was held. One of their desks remained with, of all delightful surprises, their pin-ups under the cover - undamaged, dated and perfect. The elegance, the hats, the dresses! No approach without a deep bowing, feathered hat in hand, would have been acceptable.

The voluminous desk, open, displays Victorian seam-stitch, embroidered fichus, chemises, finely tucked nightdresses, and exquisite lace. On the wall above hangs a large marriage settlement on vellum, framed in gilded gold, and dated 1686. The wide desk has a kneehole on one side only. The first document beautifully scripted would have been placed on one side while the student created an exact transcript for the indenture.

In the centre of the floor stands the first fire engine the town possessed, presented in 1761 by the Viscount (as then) Mount Edgcumb M.P. On four solid wheels, with two lead-painted tanks for water, the whole was manhandled into position. Two men dragged at front, two braked at rear. Water found from stream, well or trough was pumped twenty five feet by four men working in time. An American remarked that he thought someone would have come to meet them saying "forget it." Young boys delight in manning the pumps.

Exhibits are so shown that one may touch or lightly handle them. Following is a display of miners' tools and spears, sword blades, bullets and shot flasks dug up around-about. Many date from the Civil War. One treasured loan is a shining brass kettle on a brass stand as used in the coaches. The stand is hollow to contain an iron block. This was removed and heated red hot (as were box irons) by the landlord while horses were being changed. Hot grog could then be brewed within the coach. Judging from the journal of a wool-clothier in the town, a coach reached London from Plymouth in three days.

Oddments containing history continue to appear, such as Billy Bray's lantern. A fighting dog's collar disclosed that a bull, and at times a bear, were in Monmouth Square for baiting by dogs. By offering a penny one could have two swipes at the bull oneself. Such items come to light from journals.

There is a good selection of farm tools such as a spading iron for boots, a clyster for "stoppages" and various traps.

In a tall glass-fronted cupboard is a sewing machine identical with the earliest one in the Science Museum, 1872, both achieving only chain-stitch. A child's Gainsborough bonnet, 1757, an elaborate nightcap, a smoking cap and a handwoven sheet made from home-grown flax for a great grandmother's wedding in 1906.

Some curiosities in china made in our potteries, such as a large loving cup made for the original Talbot Hotel, stand beside a pair of Kitchener jugs.

The river has produced bottles, pottery and cannon balls.

A two foot high statue of the Duke of Wellington made in the iron foundry at St. Blazoy stands over a fine piece of Luxulyanite of which his tomb in St. Paul's is built. The Duke stood as M.P. for Mitchell for a few years. Nearby a block of iron from our short lived mine stands beside a block of tin. These two call forth squeaks of astonishment from young people when asked to handle, on discovering that tin weighs the heavier.

A press gang warrant dated 1795 written in a fine thin hand is framed and protected by blue tissue. An exact reproduction in Gothic script by our expert labeller, quotes the search for "disorderly persons, rogues and vagabonds between the ages 15-50."

An outbreak of cholera in 1853 brought massively worded regulations from the Mayor, to warn against 'the pestiferous battery.' "Every defective drain is a cholera magasine. It revels in a drunkard's cup. Avoid excess in Public houses. In private dwell as you would avoid the withering blast of this pestilence. The cholera gambols in gaseous bubbles." During the outbreak the Stannary prison was used to isolate sufferers.

Below a table, a copper meat dish cover twenty two inches long with an ornamental handle leads one to confess, to remembering one of the dinner table with a fourteen inch long crested gravy spoon! Beside is a Victorian footbath and the ubiquitous dipper, which answered every purpose. Also on the floor is an elaborately painted Victorian lavatory bowl found in the Squire's town house.

The towns prison remains as used, with rough stone floor and iron grating at the window. Prisoners hung their boots outward pleading for a drink. The original chain with ankle stocks gives a warning.

In an attic since 1865 was a crinoline, preserved as worn. For safety the treasure stays hung from the ceiling. The waist measures sixteen inches. As yet no visitor has qualified! Can one be surprised at the frequent resort to vinaigrette?

A lantern with horn for lights is undated. A grandfather clock, the face designed in the town, is beside a complete genealogical table of the Mount Edgcumbe family.

One find from an outhouse and kindly granted to the museum is an early Georgian cooking stove. The meat hung to roast on bars before the barred open fire, where wood was the fuel. The fire could be four feet wide or by means of handles, could be reduced to two feet. A moveable stand at either end took kettle or saucepan. Under the roasting bar, one could draw out three circular holders for pots, which one imagines caught the fat from the roasts. The origin of the word dripping?

A cloam oven would have been needed for baking. We still hope to obtain an example; but when extricated, being so brittle with use, they invariably fall in many pieces.

On a wall we have the whole of "Kernow bys vyken" in inch-high white lettering on black background paper. Two girls from

Brittany were studying this for fifteen minutes. They turned round saying, "We can read every word." Hearing this a visitor turned, "Oh, so you are French?" Instantly they drew themselves up. "No, we are Bretons."

Beneath the window a large case contains small treasures, one of which is the smallest and most precious exhibit, a small silver coin dated 1341. In 1339 the Black Prince paid Scottish archers and Welsh spearmen 2d. a day to come down to Cornwall. They camped on the hills awaiting the essay into France. In 1946 the hill land was in flower fields; a picker exclaimed, "I have found a coin!" "No," returned the others, "It's only a bottle top. We often find them." However, the finder thought otherwise. The coin was identified by Mr. Douch as under King David IV of Scotland, 1341. Displayed here are monogrammed seals, china, a truncheon and a large hatpin, both of which one now thinks of as weapons, also small interesting antiques. This case is the only untouchable selection of treasures. Highly valued by the owner and by many visitors are two copies of the Times. One reporting Trafalgar, the other, the Battle of Waterloo. In the Times for November 7th, 1805, there is a first hand account of the end of Nelson by Admiral Collingwood. That evening Covent Garden produced a hasty and elegant compliment to the memory of Lord Nelson. Also the advertisements give a fascinating picture, with the word respectable included in each, whether for an amanuensis, a wet nurse or an under laundry maid.

In the original copy of the Times for June 22nd, 1815, reporting Waterloo, the main report is from the Duke of Wellington himself. He describes the battle and mentions with praise for and regret the severe wounding of Col. Sir William de Lancey, great-great-uncle of the writer. He "conceived that his wound was mortal." When soldiers came to raise him, he said "Leave me and attend to those men who will live to fight again for their country."

These advertisements are even more enlightening. Both papers have been covered in fixable cellophane. They are thus clearly readable and indestructable.

Finally, Victorian Valentine cards in a frame, and an album of old photographs of town personalities, often as children. These are a source of glee to visiting relations.

A few exhibits leave one regretful. A street sign 'Tangier' showed which part of the town produced volunteers for the war under Charles II. One of the King's natural sons stationed in Plymouth, received orders to enlist, "disorderly persons, rogues and vagabonds" for the wars. Those from the town had a street named in their honour. Very regrettably the Town Council altered the road to

Castle Street, rebuffing the name with interest and history. The "Castle" referred to, is a folly, built as were follies, to aggrandise the the position of the owner.

One may perhaps draw from this description that the simplest findings give the most unexpected pleasure. There is something to interest all ages. Everything has been identified and as nearly as possible, dated. Exhibits have been sent to the British Museum, the Naval Museum at Greenwich and the Victoria and Albert Museum for confirmation. An example was a head carved in stone, dug in the garden of an important person in the parish and claimed as historical and Grecian. After ten days the British Museum confirmed not only was it not genuine but it was possibly made as a tourist market attraction.!

A silver goblet, claimed as dug up near Restormel Castle, was found to have Victorian silver markings!

Four wild life cases give surprise and pleasure to young people. While opening for ten days at Easter, the museum is without fail open from 10.15 - 12.30 and 2.00 - 4.30 from early May - September 30th and welcomes any donations.

A DELIGHT AT HARROW BARROW

If you walk through the village of Harrow Barrow near Callington, you will see out of the corner of an eye a garden lawn well above road level. There, before his cottage window, a Cornish builder has created a miniature church, a millhouse, a set of Cornish cottages and a model of Jamaica Inn. Each stands barely two feet high, and is perfect in every detail.

The church is of light stone with two slated aisles and a tower with low pinnacles, as in so many Cornish churches. The windows are Gothic and mullioned.

The millhouse and mill wheel, which one may set to work, is a water wheel, complete with a barn for storing the grain after crushing. The model of Jamaica Inn has the long low inn building, with stables at one side, and a walled courtyard before the Inn. These windows are narrow and mullioned, with shutters. Each stone in the building is set in separately, the whole being in perfect proportion.

The two cottages are built after the old fashion, with a stone porch, and windows each with nine small lights. The chimneys are three tiered with slate drips as in cottages built in a valley. Many a chimney in the Tamar valley is eight feet high. The angle of the slated roof is cleverly concave and uneven as are the old roofs. Adjoining each cottage is a low house for a pig or fowls. The builder has for all grateful and appreciative people founded a lasting reminder of buildings that we shall soon find only in an unmodernised Cornish village.

RABBIT BOXES

Many estates in Cornwall have several acres of woodland where hen pheasants nest beneath stone hedges where the sun warms their backs. The cock bird helps in the choice of a site. The keeper knows the nests and gradually collects the eggs for hatching in batteries or under broody hens. They are reared in the gameparks which are surrounded by stone hedging five to six feet high. In this stone walling there are what appears to be drain holes at regular intervals of eight to twelve feet. But on going closer, one sees the holes are well constructed tunnels about twelve inches high, running through the stone hedge. The inside is roughly paved, and roofed with flat stone. Three stones form the entrance, one horizontal held up by two upright, well bonded into the walling. The tunnels are about fifteen inches from the ground, and run through to a like entrance inside the park. Old men knew them as "rabbit boxes."

Through the boxes rabbits could come and go. In spite of their sins rabbits had some valuable assets. All the tender shoots of brambles were nipped almost literally in the bud by their chewing. Thus the woods were kept clear of undergrowth. Now woodlands, unless of beech, are almost impassable unless one is attired in leggings or wellingtons.

Rabbits could thus enter and leave the game parks without game escaping. Nor did they need to undermine the walls to gain the park. No game birds would venture into a dark tunnel, even though it was lit from without.

If the waller or tenant fancied a rabbit for dinner, he had only to set a gin trap in the hole without fear of capturing a game bird. Many present owners of estates, who have gained them by acquisition rather than inheritance, regard the rabbit boxes as drain holes to this day!

LANLIVERY PARISH
FARMING & ESTATE IN 19th CENTURY - EARLY 20th CENTURY

In Cornwall, where estates did not run into thousands of acres, and where there were none of the distractions of city life, landowners lived on a congenial footing with their tenant farmers. The eternal seasons dominated both their lives. Their pleasures were shared. They met on equal terms in the hunting field; the farmers joined in the gambling of the cock-pits, having often bred the winning birds. Allowances were made for the deprivations of game. In a good year, game was distributed. In poor years, arrears in rent were allowed to lapse, sometimes for an indefinite period.

Though paternalism was perhaps evident, there was neighbourliness, consideration and above all diginity on both sides.

LANLIVERY

Lanlivery is a small country parish of fifteen square miles in mid-Cornwall. For over 30 years, the sole occupation of the parish has been farming.

Families live in farmhouses and cottages occupied for generations by their respective and respected ancestors. A bond of sharing and comparing, of neighbourly understanding and tolerance of the various family ways and traditions has bred a delightfully integrated and unpretentious community.

Geographically, Lanlivery is a microcosm of Cornwall. A granite ridge road bisects the parish from east to west. The land above the ridge sloping northerly is light, with granite subsoil; the land below, sloping southerly, is fertile, loamy and sheltered.

Here in almost equal parts, are the four kinds of terrain found in Cornwall:-

(a) Hilly with granite subsoil.
(b) Moorland and marsh.
(c) Hilly, well farmed, heavy mineral subsoil.
(d) Sheltered valleys, mild, wooded, very fertile.

There is even a small area of blue slate named "Delabole," and four acres named "Tin Park" on Penpell Farm.

The highest point is 685 ft. The water table flows from Helman's Tor, in the north-east, standing at 675 ft. Fast-flowing streams run into the Fowey river, and acres of moorland lie at the foot of the Tor.

In 1814 the population was:-

Males	Females	Inhabited Houses
607	640	240
Other Buildings		Uninhabited Houses
3		15

Death rate in 1814 in an adjoining parish (Population: 374)

Infants under 1	Childbed	Fever	Smallpox
60	5	25	15
T. B.	Accident	Other Causes	
10	3	2	

THE VILLAGE

The Church stands central and proud at 615 ft. In 1816 an order from the Bishop of Exeter granted £121 to be paid quarterly to the curate of Lanlivery, increasing to £131 in 1870 and to £150 in 1877. With tithes at 1/- to 1/6 in the £1 on the 25 farms in the parish, and payment by the Crown of 5/- a year to whitewash the tower as a landmark to sailors, the parsons enjoyed a healthy living.

A square granite building near the Church is the Reading Room; opposite was the Smithy, below stands an Elizabethan vicarage with stabling; above stands the School, founded by the Kendall family, the largest landowner, in whose gift is the incumbency.

The small village store and Post Office stands above the Crown Inn, and Churchtown Farm across the road had one field designated as the "Bowling Green."

Readings and simple concerts were held weekly in the Reading Room, people young and old walking many miles through dark lanes, the girls carrying lanterns.

LANDOWNERS

1841. The Kendall family, owners of the Manor of Polhorman, owned nineteen farms. The Hon. Anna Maria Gar of Lanhydrock, owned five farms. Richard Foster of Lanwithian owned one.

TENURE

1800. Land was leased for a period of lives, usually three lives - the longest liver being determined by the taker - or alternatively for 99 years, or in the case of tenements for 999 years.

TENANCIES

Tenancies were of three kinds:-

Free Tenants - farms capable of maintenance to the full by the tenant (few).

Rack Tenants - farms for which the owner provided the fixed capital, the tenant the working capital (the majority).

Conventionary Tenants - literally those farms where the tenants followed the convention of lease for lives, and paid renewal fines or heriots on charges of lives.

On the Kendall estate, the heriot rarely exceeded £1 or £2. Failing money, the heriot could be paid in kind e.g. best beast or capon, value 1/- to 2/-. The tithe Commutation Acts, 1839 forbade payment in kind.

RENTALS

Rentals were held at the Crown Inn, half-yearly, at Lady Day and Michaelmas and were collected and entered in copperplate hand in a large leather-covered rental. Honesty was particularly expected of a Steward.

There were often arrears, and allowances for damage by rabbits, or for woodland planting, or for rack tenants repairs or needs. In 1839 when a farmer died, £15 arrears of rent was given to the widow and the rent reduced from £50 to £45.

In 1843 Trevethy - allowance for land taken in by railway £1.3.1.

1845. PELYN LAWN

Pelyn was the house of the Kendalls, the lawn fields and mill let at Rack rent. Presumably the tenant cared for the horses.

Bill for wheat.	£24.14.0d.
Allowance for keep of horses	4.0s.0d.
Allowance for damage by rabbits	11.0s.0d.
To improve dwelling hse.	10.0s.0d.
For want (sic.) of thresh machine	5.0s.0d.
Land taken for road (drive)	5s.0d
Land taken for planting 2 yrs. at 15/-	1.10s.0d.
Bill for shoeing, etc.	99.4s.5½d.

1847. TRETHEW (RACK)

18 Caps & posts at 20d.	£1.10s.0d.
Pump	1.0s.0d.
Pigs & pump troughs	1.11s.3d.
Salting trough	16s.0d.
Round trough	5s.0d.
22 perch of wall	1.14s.4d.

1849. An Entry of Rental Expenses

Rents amounted to   £1093.14s.0d.

Paid Court Expenses £8.10s.7d.

Received of

Conventionary tenants	2. 0s.0d.
	6.10s.7d.
Gig Hire	11s.6d.
	7. 2s.1d.

Rental received   £1086.11s.11d.

N.B. The punctilious honesty of the steward to the last penny! As part of Court Expenses, the usual custom of allowing 2/6d. to each farmer for his dinner and loss of time - would have been followed.

HERIOTS & FINES

The heriots appear often to be inequitable, e.g.

On a child 3 yrs	£3	rent	£2. 9s.8d.
On a child 13 yrs.	6/8d.	rent	12s.6d.
Daughter 14 yrs.	£1	rent	£1. 0s.0d.
Daughter 11 yrs.	3/4d.	rent	1s.6d.

Were they larger or better land? Heriots were stated and entered at each rental, e.g.

Ben Sturtridge -	
Wife Uzella	54
Eliza daughter	34
Richard son	28

Heriot 5/-   Rent 10/-

"Amerciament" is an occasional entry - a fine or penalty inflicted by the court e.g. 2/-. The Courts Baron inflicted fines as follows:-

1) Breaking field with horses without consent
2) Making a highway in common pasture
3) Breaking common in May after sunrise

Penalty 2/- to Lord of Manor

1/- to driver.

LEASES

Four conditions governed farm leases.
1) A fifth of the farm to be in grass
2) To sand the land
3) To cut wood in season
4) To repair thatch roofs

ASSESSMENT OF RENT
1811

Four conditions determined rents.
1) Aspect - land facing or sloping to the south and/or west produced earlier crops and grass than would north and/or east.
2) Quality of soil - whether loam, tough or turfy, granite subsoil or hilly.
3) Vicinity to sand - the only land improver used in any quantity by every farmer.
4) Vicinity to market town - a considerations with tolls and large tracks wearisome to man and beast.

1811 LAND WAS ASSESSED AS FOLLOWS:-

Park 6/- acre - (near farmhouse, sheltered)
Meadow 5/- acre - in proportion to arable
Arable 4/6d. acre - the greater part
Moor pasture 3/- - included marsh
Hilly 2/6d. - entailing work in carrying soil to top in slides
Waste land provided furze, turf and summer feed and was un-titheable
1850. Permanent pasture, when so marked on deeds (on deeds and maps as p.p.) was land that in the quittal of the tenant, must be left as taken over, i.e. in the rich pasturable state. There was seldom interference here, as the old saying 'to break a pasture makes a man; to make a pasture breaks a man' holds true. On p.p. it would appear, that herbs or grasses of medicinal value to livestock have become permanent, so that a free range stock will always return to permanent pasture during a part of each day.

In this survey of farming and estate in the parish of Lanlivery in the 19th and early 20th centuries there is much evidence of the good relations existing between landowners and tenants. As may be deduced from the appended letter written to his solicitors, Nicholas Kendall, the largest landowner, was a considerate and generous squire. With other members of the landed gentry, he might well have expressed the drawing to a close of years of good management and mutual respect in the following words written in 1910. "We, who are owners, have done our best to act as if in partnership with our tenants, and have not been governed by purely mercenary considerations; we find now that other sources of income must regulate our affairs."

FARMING IN CORNWALL IN THE NINETEENTH CENTURY

FARMHOUSES

The farmhouses stand in their original positions, on land sheltered by rising ground behind and having water nearby. They face south or west and were at the outset built of cob or thatched, later of killas or freestone.

The windows usually overlook the farmyard; the farmer's eye must always be on the alert. Indeed, many dislike doors closed indoors, feeling perhaps cut off from livestock. Floors are earthen or flagstone, or, later, slate. The roof is concave. The walls are freestone, the windowsills slate. Rats have at times entered cavity walls from stables and raced round rooms and under floors, like a pack of hounds. In the early years of the nineteenth century there were six or seven outbuildings:-

1) Cow house for six or eight cows and calving pen.
2) Stables.
3) Barn and wood chamber, above ox or bullock house.
4) Turnip house - to store and cut up root crops.
5) Vealing house - dark for calf-rearing to produce white flesh.
6) Small pig houses, with pig pen.
7) Threshing house - where corn was threshed by tramping horses.

PLAN OF FARMHOUSE IN 1940. Lower Demesmes - Lanlivery.
DOOMSDAY

Kitchen 6ft. 10ins. - Ceiling boarded, board having groove with tongue separate. Hand-made nails. Lintels of doors, branches, bark adhering and curving in natural wood. Hearth fire and cloam oven. Chimney with huge oak beam and chains for pots.

Small front room. 7ft. high. - Thin oak boarding partition. Outer wall 4ft. thick, turf rubble and shard centre. Back wall 7ft. thick.

Bedrooms. - 3 above house, 2 attic, above lean-to.

FARMING FAMILIES

Beside his family a farmer would house a working girl, sometimes a working lad, and usually one or two children from a tenement family, ostensibly as apprentices. Seven surnames occur through generations holding the same tenancies in Lanlivery. From 1814: Littleton, W. & J. Wherry, Dunn, Rundle, Phillips, Treleaven and Higgs.

1818. A will made by William Rowe
"I give and bequeath to my wife Jane Rowe, the bed we usually sleep in with stead and furniture thereunto belonging, which she is, can or otherwise might be entitled to - and my will is that the Albion Insurance Co. if paid and contributed equally to annual premium, to be to sole and separate use of my said daughter and not to be subject to the debts or control disposition or engagement of her present or any future husband."

LABOUR
The year's work was seasonally governed.

AUTUMN
Ploughing - 1 acre per day
Burnish arishes
Root crops in clamps
Hedging and faggoting

WINTER
Bullock in houses - fed and watered four times daily
Calves under cover
Turnip and mangolds chopped by hand
Pig-killing.

SPRING
Dressing carried out to fields and 'skoded'
Seedlips used for sowing and manuring
Lambing

SUMMER
Fresh grass in May
Shearing - dipping
Harvest

1811. A farm servant, man, received 8-12 guineas a year and board.
Maid 3-4 guineas a year and board.
A Labourer 9/- week and corn, ground for bread.
Women 6d. a day from 6a.m. - 6p.m. in winter from dawn to dusk. At harvest, meat and drink were provided. Cutting corn and hay, 2/6d. acre and gallon cider.

In 1907 - personal memory. A line of men scything in rhythm; two boys with wooden rakes, raking the corn into bundles. Two young women binding the sheaves. At the far end of the field children and grandmother busy gleaning every ear of corn and even grains left lying to drop them in a large tin bath.

After a day or two of gleaning, sows and geese were loosed to complete the good work.

1806. APPRENTICES. From 1806 - 1813 boys and girls as young as 7 and 8 years were sent for no payment, to yeoman farmers, where they lived as the family ostensibly until 21 or the year of marriage. They are immortalised in nursery rhyme as little Boy Blue, Mary and

the Piper's son, etc. They rarely left their own parish and were overseen and undersigned by two magistrates. By 1814, the children were apprenticed rather older, at twelve to fourteen years. From 1818-1835 Nicholas Kendall, Squire was an assenting magistrate. 1830. An example of the overseers work.
"To W. Littleton, Chark - a complaint on behalf of Jos. Treleaven, who did recently receive parish pay 1/6 a week - now received 1d only. He is old, infirm and destitute, his allowance is again raised to 1/6. He cannot provide necessaries for less. If wanting, clothing should be supplied."

W. Littleton already had three apprenticed children of nine, eight and ten. The unbroken line of Littletons were farming Chark in 1979.

FOOD

1820. The farmers ate meat and wheaten bread. Labourers ate barley bread, salt fish, and natural food in season. Cows were let out to the poor at 6d. each. The hirer paid the cow-rent in milk and butter. Scald milk went to his family and reared the pig and calf.The owner received half the calf price. This mutual undertaking takes place today,with sheep rented out, the farmer taking half value of lambs, known as 'out to half-crease.'
1915. I remember seeing a cottage woman open her door and hand a thick slice of bread to each of her two children, with the words "go and find some blackberries," their dinner!
1880. One farmer's son carried to school every day a pasty filled with boiled rice and currants. He was hale and well at 90! Watercress and bacon was a favourite filling. Kettle broth - boiled water poured over bread, butter, herbs and seasoning.
1860. A pig was killed in late autumn and salted in granite trough. If killed when 'in season,' the bacon was unfit, shiny and would not keep.
1920. Pilchards split and cooked on grill over an open fire, sputter fat, and flames frizzle the small bones - an ideal method. Only one farm - Trethew - had a 'culver park' denoting an erstwhile pigeon house.

FUEL

1811. In 1811, fuol in Cornwall was turf or peat and furze to heat the cloam ovens. Faggots were burned on the open hearths. When Welsh coal and the Cornish stove came in , it was lit only from 10 a.m. - 2 p.m. to cook the midday meal. Other cooking was done on the brandis (a trivet) or under a baker (an iron dome) on the hearth.

1907. Cow pats were used as fuel. Presumably when feed became richer the pats would disintegrate.

MARKET, TOLLS, POUND HOUSES

1814. The Market town nearest to Lanlivery was, and is, Lostwithiel. They were held once a month in Markethouse Street (Queen St.), which has a raised bank above it, where stall-holders set up their wares. Cows and calves, bullocks, sheep, ponies, horses and carts carrying pigs, men shouting, sticks waving, thronged the street as far as Restormel Road. The noise and confusion would have been unimaginable. There were two toll bars, as marked on the map. One at the junction of the Fowey road and the road from the West. One at the junction of the road from Lanlivery and the road from Bodmin. Both tolls led to Lostwithiel.

TOLL CHARGES

1814. Waggon 1/6d., Bullocks 10d. a score. Pigs and sheep less, but pigs and calves would have been taken by cart, with a covering rope net. Near each toll-bar was a pound horse, and two acre field. Tolls were collected for the Commissioners of Turnpike Roads and the Turnpike Trustees.

Farmers were to keep roads in repair. Bye-roads were rough, dark and labyrinthine and bridges merely stepping stones.

FARMS AMALGAMATED DURING 19th CENTURY

1850. There were in several cases farms of the same name, Higher and Lower. Of these it is invariably the Higher where the dwelling house is no longer used as such, but serves as a barn or shelter. The reason would probably be that the Higher, being thus on poorer land, was less profitable.

FARMS BUILT UP

1860. Alternatively four or five farms have been acquired piecemeal. The rents were high, as the small fields of which they were made up, were either near market, e.g. Bodardle or in demand for cottagers ponies, cow or use, e.g. Poldhu.

TITHES AND POOR RATES

The vicar received tithes of 1/- in £1, collected vicariously by tithe collectors. At harvest, Church claimed the tenth sheaf, also the tenth sucking pig. Farmers were notified when the harvest was in hand, or when a sow farrowed. Incumbents made use of glebe land. Taxes were levied on farmers for the roads. Taxes for militia and seamen were raised. The Poor Law rates were usually left for women to produce from carding and spinning.

FARMING PROCEDURE
Implements

Waggons, wains (for sheaves), dung pots (carried on pony), plough harrow, wood seed-lip (for sowing seed or sand). Plough for oxen or one horse.

Tools

Biddix = pickaxe. Yewell = fork, long-handled, 4 prongs. Cornish shovel for hedging.

Livestock

Cows, bullocks, oxen, horses, sheep and pigs.

Sheep - Border Leicester - prone to twin lambs, South Devon - close wool.

Bullocks - only grew to 3-5 cwt. and were either sent to Somerset to fatten or sent to Plymouth for the Navy.

Pigs - were fed on scald milk and used to clean potato and harvest fields.

1858. TRADES SERVING FARMERS

In Lostwithiel - Maltster for barley.	
Cordwainer (Barrow)	harness and repairs
Cooper (Burroughs)	barrels, mill buckets and handles
Saddlers (Beckereleg)	
Coach Builders (Eastlick)	carts and repairs and wheelwright
Chandler (Beswarick)	corn and wool merchant
Wool Merchant	Tangier wool store
Tallow mongers	

1827. Smith - besides shoeing, endless repairs, e.g.

Bonding wheel	1/-
Mending Yewell	3d.
Pig rings	1d. each
Lying (welding)	
Plough shares and coulter	3/-
Chimney bar	2/-
2 shoes	1/-

COURSE OF CROPS
Crops followed a five year plan.
Turnip, barley, wheat, barley, oats and seeds. Wheat was steeped, seed was broadcast by man carrying seedlip, or latter by woman with a seeding paddle. Wheat reaped with hooks, and grown for thatch. Barley scythed and maled. Stubble was raked and 'arrish' burned in small heaps, a sight and sign of autumn. Hoeing was begun at this time, the Swedish turnip was introduced. Potatoes were found to be suited to Cornish soil and climate. After the five year cycle of crops, two years follow. Permanent pasture took five years to attain. Fields for hay had to have livestock withdrawn by Christmas previous.

MANURE
Sand was the sole land improver. Each village had its 'sandy way,' the road or lane leading most directly to the shore. Seeweed would be heaped on earth heaps, covered by sand and road sweepings and scrapings later 'skoded' and ploughed in. News of a catch of dog-fish sent farmers hastening for a load.

HEDGE ENCLOSURE
Enclosures on the northern farms were of stone, capped with earth or turf. Stone was abundant, and cleavage understood - walls firm set by time, stand to this day as built in 1750 to comply with the Enclosure acts. In the Southern farms, earth crevices have filled with plants and bushes rooted on the cope. These hedges need more maintenance, being cut and plashed. Stone hedging was at the rate of 10/- for 18ft. and 6ft. high. Gates were of oak, 15/- with posts.

WATER
Lanlivery is a well-watered parish, streams and springs abound. Water, with shelter were the primary considerations in siting a farm and the dwelling house. In the latter half of the 19th century, water mills were built for corn grinding. Seven mills sited throughout the parish sufficed to serve all farms. Regulated by sluices; triut lived in the millpools. Word flew round when 'millpools draining' and children ran with baskets to scoop the fish. Mill buckets were of wood, banded with leather and tarred.

BYE-PRODUCTS
Tallow - the hides of the small bullocks produced much tallow.
Hoofs and Trotters - boiled down in cauldrons for glue - a profitable

line.

Wood - oak was grown for the tanners. A tanhouse at Lostwithiel.
Charred oak was sent to blowing house, on Redmoor in North-East
Willow and Ash were planted for coopers.

No toll bar to market.

1968. Present rent £4 an acre. £175.

FIELD NAMES

Byng - probably a rickfield or yard and/or storage clamp. Large
farms had upper byng, four large byngs and byng - as Trethevy and
Stickstenton, both with southerly slope and therefore sheltered
corn.

Goom and Goomer - a cart-house or implement shed.

Bee Park - probably beef park.

Cold Harbour - probably treed, i.e. col d'arbre.

Quillet - a strip often 1 furlong   1 furlong long.

Bottoms - low ground - marsh or wet coppice.

Skeer -

Demesnes of Manor - scattered strips.

ENDING

As may be deduced from the enclosed letter written to his
solicitors, Nicholas Kendall was a considerate and generous landowner. With other members of the landed gentry, he might well
have expressed the drawing to a close years of good management
and mutual respect in the following words, written in 1910.

"We, who are owners, have done our best to act as if in
partnership with our tenants and have not been governed by purely
mercenary considerations; find now that other sources of income
must regulate our affairs."

AN ESTATE ACCOUNT BOOK
1623 - 1696

In the spring of 1970 there was a detailed description of farming in
Lanlivery parish during the 19th and early 20th centuries in the
Federation magazine. I have now had the delight of going through an
estate account book of the same parish dated from 1622 - a mere 200
years earlier.

The book was found behind panelling at the side of a back

stairway. It is long and narrow, the sheepskin binding brown with age, stiff and crackling. Fine strips of leather tie it to threads of string round the leaves. A tie of leather held it closed at top and bottom. The tanned knobbly leather cover still gleams, though the corners of the pages are rolled back and the spine broken. The parchment-like leaves are held together with fine string. Each leasf has to be eased out of the tightly furled up corners at the lower ends.

Could one find paper now that would endure being wholly covered on both sides with the scratchings of a quill pen and remain perfectly legible after 350 years? At times the ink was unworthy of the paper, or even of the goose quill carefully pruned with a penknife. On some leaves the faint blur of ink entries earlier is written over with entries of twenty years later.

The Squire's life comes to light from day to day. Queries chase one another through one's mind. How did he cope with the endless capons dealt out to him? How did he find his way through his account book? One leaf will carry an entry at the foot dated 1647; above it there will perhaps be two entries dated 1657 and 1659! What course was taken with a tenant who contributed nothing on rent days, when the others have a cross for every quarter over two years? Who was the moorsman, never named, who took charge of cattle sent to him? And what gave rise to the curious wager with Bishop Trelawney? If one turns every leaf, deciphering the 17th century handwriting and taking in sequence examples of the various rents, agreements, memos and even wagers, one gains much enlightenment on one way of life in 17th century Cornwall.

Nicholas Kendall succeeded his father in 1623. He was then 28 and married to Emeline, daughter of Thomas Treffry. Presumably it was with great pride that he opened his first account book.

1623 (headed Anno Domini 1623) there then follow three leaves entirely given over to the description of his fighting cocks, their special markings and the names of tenants and farms where they were sent for rearing. It is hoped to record this at a later date. One feels, from the scarcity of Nicholas Kendall's entries, that his interests lay outside the management of his estate. Walter Kendall, his heir in 1642 was absorbed in the Manor.

Walter Kendall succeeded his father. At first, being only 20, he was hesitant but, as he acquired confidence, the manor was run with enterprise. He married Jane, daughter of Sir Alexander Carew, Bt. of Antony in 1650, but the marriage was childless.

1642. In a beautiful copperplate hand the rent roll is entered. "Michaelmas quarter 1642.

Conventionary Tenants.

Walter Maynard	0-8-10
John Leane	0-3-4
Peter Hornabrooke	0-5-0-
John Hawking	0-5-0 and 20 others"

Free tenants were capable of maintaining the farm to the full. Conventionary tenants held the lease on the convention of 'lives,' usually three. They paid a heriot or renewal fee on change of lives. On the Kendall estate these amounted to £2 or £3; or the lord of the manor would declare himself "content with a best beast," often a cow.

1650. "That most of the tenancies have made a compact to pay for three plowing journeys and garrowing three shillings and fower pence, the agreement being made at the court held unto Polharmon the same day witness me Walter Kendall, Lord of the sayd mannor." Let us remember this was the year of his wedding, hence the pride of position perhaps!

1650. "Paid of capons and plowing journeys at Mich: quarter as follows / David hirst pl: - 2 - garr: - 1 - capons - 2 / Rich: Bodye pl: 1 - capons 3." These tenants would have ploughed and harrowed land counted in days and were then paid in capons. The trafficking in capons, to and fro, leaves one bewildered.

1651. "Memo that Will: (short for William) Clarke owing all his capons for ye yere '51. Jane Clarke paid 12s for her father Will Clarke it being in full satisfaction of all capons dew unto Mich: 1651." On the line above is "Jane brought for her father 4 capons." And so the entries continue all down the page. Countless capons change hands, invariably either way for one shilling each. Were they actual capons or was this the accepted name for any cockerel? A tenant was expected to work two or three days for the Lord of the manor at harvest and was generally paid a few shillings, instead of an extra rent if he failed to give this service.

1652. At this time the squire began to erect mills and property in Lostwithiel. William Taprell became tenants of the malthouse on which a granite lease stone bears the inscription on the quoin:-

"Walter Kendall was funder of this house 1658
Hath a lease for 3 thousand yeres which hath
beginning 29 Sept 1652."

This rent, 12s. a quarter, came under "quillets and

41

tenements." The lane alongside is still known as Tapprell Lane.

1653. "Ladye (Lady Day presumably) / Those have payd their plowing and garrowing and capons and harvest journeys / Symon Bonny - 2-0 / John Keane capons - 2-0, plow and garr: 3-6 / Peter Hornabrooke capons - 2-0 / John Taprell being 5 capons 10-0 / John Loane cap 2-0 plow and carriage 2-6." and so on. May we not imagine Squire, his "fair round belly with good capon lin'd?"

One wonders whether, with the end of the Civil War, lessons had been learned and improvements born, as sand now appears in massive quantities for the land. The Kendalls took part in the war and, passing through other lands, would have realised that Cornwall, with her granite subsoil, had sheer need of fertilising and balancing with added calcium. Cow pats lacking richness, did not disintegrate; they were soon gathered up to be used as fuel. Manure heaps were composed of dog fish or seaweed, sand and soil and road sweepings. The heap was turned over several times.

The Kendalls did not frequent the Court seeking titles. Their interests lay in their lands and their tenants. They were generous land lords.

1664. "payd unto Matthew Sambles of the mannor of Bodardle for onant rent for Penquite high rent and suit of court 0-7-6 / 0-1-6." The suit of court befell him because he did not attend in person.

"Ye 15 June. The mending of ye barn and ye making of ye mill pool." The mill refers to a mill built beside the river in Lostwithiel, used until the coming of electricity, of latter years by Cornwall Farmers. A granite quoin has the initials W.K.

Having before mentioned the somewhat haphazard arrangements of Squire's accounts, I cannot resist including this entry:-

"3 of August 1678: I cannot find the last. In truth the hole money is payd."

There now follows the most unexpected entry of all. The Bishop implicated is Trelawney who was then Bishop of Bristol.

"Memo that the Bishop of Bristow had of me one guinea upon condition that if his Ladye be not with child within the yere from yt day he is to pay me twentye guinneys and yt she is not as present with child or if a month she bee, then I am to have my wageing. In presence of Mr. Sheriffe, Sir John Carew, Sir J. Arundel and others this contract was made."

As the signature of the following entry is that of a name quite unheard of in the neighbourhood, one wonders what led to the unmistakeable air of exasperation that pervades the whole. The handwriting except for the signature is that of Walter Kendall. It reads thus:- "Received then of Walter Kendall of Pelyn in full of all account reckonings dew or pretented to be dew from ye beginning of ye world unto this day the summ of 0-15-0. Signed Henry Kingsbury, witness to this William Oliphant, Thomas Gaved."

1692. "25 of IOber (presumably October): Received of Roger Thomas in full for Great Colligeen rent the sum of 0-7-8 and allowed him for all accounts dew to this time and he is to pay thi yere's rent being dew this Xmas unto 1693 unto Mrs. Mary Kendall witness our hands Walter Kendall, Roger Thomas." Mary Kendall was buried in Henry VII chapel, Westminster Abbey, 'for her devout and Godly life.'

1694. After many transactions over wool lasting over eight years he always chose Thomas Gaved as witness. There are numerous entries thus:- "18th of 8ber: payd Tomas Gaved for one quarters wages now dew 1-0-0." Perhaps a personal servant always at hand. A large scrawling signature, it sufficed.

1694. "29 of May: Received of Noath Naniulian of Luxilian for a heriot dew upon ye death of Ann Clarke." Walter Kendall was now approaching 74 years. The handwriting becomes less steady and, at the end of the year following, there is the final entry which closes the book.